John Smith, U.S.A. by Eugene Field

Eugene Field was born on 2nd September 1850 in St. Louis, Missouri. His mother died when he was six and his father when he was nineteen. His academic life was not taken seriously and he preferred the life of a prankster until, in 1875, he began work as a journalist for the St. Joseph Gazette in Saint Joseph, Missouri.

In his career as a journalist he soon found a niche that suited him. His articles were light, humorous and written in a personal gossipy style that endeared him to his readership. Some were soon being syndicated to other newspapers around the States. Field soon rose to city editor of the Gazette.

Field had first published poetry in 1879, when his poem 'Christmas Treasures' appeared. This was the beginning that would eventually number over a dozen volumes. As well as verse Field published an extensive range of short stories including 'The Holy Cross' and 'Daniel and the Devil.'

In 1889 whilst the family were in London and Field himself was recovering from a bout of ill health he wrote his most famous poem; 'Lovers Lane'.

On 4th November 1895 Eugene Field Sr died in Chicago of a heart attack at the age of 45.

Index of Contents

INTRODUCTION

From whatever point of view the character of Eugene Field is seen, genius—rare and quaint presents itself is childlike simplicity. That he was a poet of keen perception, of rare discrimination, all will admit. He was a humorist as delicate and fanciful as Artemus Ward, Mark Twain, Bill Nye, James Whitcomb Riley, Opie Read, or Bret Harte in their happiest moods. Within him ran a poetic vein, capable of being worked in any direction, and from which he could, at will, extract that which his imagination saw and felt most. That he occasionally left the child-world, in which he longed to linger, to wander among the older children of men, where intuitively the hungry listener follows him into his Temple of Mirth, all should rejoice, for those who knew him not, can while away the moments imbibing the genius of his imagination in the poetry and prose here presented.

Though never possessing an intimate acquaintanceship with Field, owing largely to the disparity in our ages, still there existed a bond of friendliness that renders my good opinion of him in a measure trustworthy. Born in the same city, both students in the same college, engaged at various times in newspaper work both in St. Louis and Chicago, residents of the same ward, with many mutual friends, it is not surprising that I am able to say of him that "the world is better off that he lived, not in gold and silver or precious jewels, but in the bestowal of priceless truths, of which the possessor of this book becomes a benefactor of no mean share of his estate."

Every lover of Field, whether of the songs of childhood or the poems that lend mirth to the out-pouring of his poetic nature, will welcome this unique collection of his choicest wit and humor.

CHARLES WALTER Brown
Chicago, January, 1905

To-day I strayed in Charing Cross as wretched as could be
With thinking of my home and friends across the tumbling sea;
There was no water in my eyes, but my spirits were depressed
And my heart lay like a sodden, soggy doughnut in my breast.
This way and that streamed multitudes, that gayly passed me by—
Not one in all the crowd knew me and not a one knew I!
"Oh, for a touch of home!" I sighed; "oh, for a friendly face!
Oh, for a hearty handclasp in this teeming desert place!"
And so, soliloquizing as a homesick creature will,
Incontinent, I wandered down the noisy, bustling hill
And drifted, automatic-like and vaguely, into Lowe's,
Where Fortune had in store a panacea for my woes.
The register was open, and there dawned upon my sight
A name that filled and thrilled me with a cyclone of delight—
The name that I shall venerate unto my dying day—
The proud, immortal signature: "John Smith, U.S.A."

Wildly I clutched the register and brooded on that name—
I knew John Smith, yet could not well identify the same.
I knew him North, I knew him South, I knew him East and West—
I knew him all so well I knew not which I knew the best.
His eyes, I recollect, were gray, and black, and brown, and blue,
And, when he was not bald, his hair was of chameleon hue;
Lean, fat, tall, short, rich, poor, grave, gay, a blonde and a brunette—
Aha, amid this London fog, John Smith, I see you yet;
I see you yet, and yet the sight is all so blurred I seem
To see you in composite, or as in a waking dream,
Which are you, John? I'd like to know, that I might weave a rhyme
Appropriate to your character, your politics and clime;
So tell me, were you "raised" or "reared"—your pedigree confess
In some such treacherous ism as "I reckon" or "I guess";
Let fall your tell-tale dialect, that instantly I may
Identify my countryman, "John Smith, U.S.A."

It's like as not you are the John that lived a spell ago
Down East, where codfish, beans 'nd bona-fide school-marms grow;
Where the dear old homestead nestles like among the Hampshire hills
And where the robin hops about the cherry boughs and trills;

Where Hubbard squash 'nd huckleberries grow to powerful size,
And everything is orthodox from preachers down to pies;
Where the red-wing blackbirds swing 'nd call beside the pickril pond,
And the crows air cawin' in the pines uv the pasture lot beyond;
Where folks complain uv bein' poor, because their money's lent
Out West on farms 'nd railroads at the rate uv ten per cent;
Where we ust to spark the Baker girls a-comin' home from choir,
Or a-settin' namin' apples round the roarin' kitchen fire:
Where we had to go to meetin' at least three times a week,
And our mothers learnt us good religious Dr. Watts to speak,
And where our grandmas sleep their sleep—God rest their souls, I say!
And God bless yours, ef you're that John, "John Smith, U.S.A."

Or, mebbe, Colonel Smith, yo' are the gentleman I know
In the country whar the finest democrats 'nd horses grow;
Whar the ladies are all beautiful an' whar the crap of cawn
Is utilized for Bourbon and true dawters are bawn;
You've ren for jedge, and killed yore man, and bet on Proctor Knott—
Yore heart is full of chivalry, yore skin is full of shot;
And I disremember whar I've met with gentlemen so true
As yo' all in Kaintucky, whar blood an' grass are blue;
Whar a niggah with a ballot is the signal fo' a fight,
Whar a yaller dawg pursues the coon throughout the bammy night;
Whar blooms the furtive 'possum—pride an' glory of the South—
And Aunty makes a hoe-cake, sah, that melts within yo' mouth!
Whar, all night long, the mockin'-birds are warblin' in the trees
And black-eyed Susans nod and blink at every passing breeze,
Whar in a hallowed soil repose the ashes of our Clay—
Hyar's lookin' at yo', Colonel "John Smith, U.S.A."!

Or wuz you that John Smith I knew out yonder in the West—
That part of our republic I shall always love the best?
Wuz you him that went prospectin' in the spring of sixty-nine
In the Red Hoss mountain country for the Gosh-All-Hemlock Mine?
Oh, how I'd like to clasp your hand an' set down by your side
And talk about the good old days beyond the big divide;
Of the rackaboar, the snaix, the bear, the Rocky Mountain goat,
Of the conversazzhyony 'nd of Casey's tabble-dote,
And a word of them old pardners that stood by us long ago
(Three-Fingered Hoover, Sorry Tom and Parson Jim, you know)!
Old times, old friends, John Smith, would make our hearts beat high again,
And we'd see the snow-top mountain like we used to see 'em then;
The magpies would go flutterin' like strange sperrits to 'nd fro,
And we'd hear the pines a-singing' in the ragged gulch below;
And the mountain brook would loiter like upon its windin' way,
Ez if it waited for a child to jine it in its play.

You see, John Smith, just which you are I cannot well recall,
And, really, I am pleased to think you somehow must be all!
For when a man sojourns abroad awhile (as I have done)
He likes to think of all the folks he left at home as one—

And so they are! For well you know there's nothing in a name—
Our Browns, our Joneses and our Smiths are happily the same;
All represent the spirit of the land across the sea,
All stand for one high purpose in our country of the free!
Whether John Smith be from the South, the North, the West, the East—
So long as he's American, it mattereth not the least;
Whether his crest be badger, bear, palmetto, sword or pine,
He is the glory of the stars that with the stripes combine!
Where'er he be, whate'er his lot, he's eager to be known,
Not by his mortal name, but by his country's name alone!
And so, compatriot, I am proud you wrote your name to-day
Upon the register at Lowe's, "John Smith, U.S.A."

THE FISHERMAN'S FEAST

Of all the gracious gifts of Spring,
Is there another can safely surpass
This delicate, voluptuous thing—
This dapple-green, plump-shouldered bass?
Upon a damask napkin laid,
What exhalations superfine
Our gustatory nerves pervade,
Provoking quenchless thirsts for wine.

The ancients loved this noble fish,
And, coming from the kitchen fire
All piping hot upon a dish,
What raptures did he not inspire!
"Fish should swim twice," they used to say—
Once in their native vapid brine,
And then a better way—
You understand? Fetch on the wine!

Ah, dainty monarch of the flood,
How often have I cast for you—
How often sadly seen you scud
Where weeds and pussy willows grew!
How often have you filched my bait!
How often have you snapped my treacherous line!—
Yet here I have you on this plate.
You shall swim twice, and now in wine!

And, harkee, garcon! let the blood
Of cobwebbed years be spilt for him—
Aye, in a rich Burgundy flood
This piscatorial pride should swim;
So, were he living, he should say
He gladly died for me and mine,
And, as it was his native spray,

He'd lash the sauce—What, ho! the wine!

I would it were ordained for me
To share your fate, oh finny friend!
I surely were not loath to be
Reserved for such a noble end;
For when old Chronos, gaunt and grim,
At last reels in his ruthless line,
What were my ecstacy to swim
In wine, in wine, in glorious wine!

Well, here's a health to you, sweet Spring!
And, prithee, whilst I stick to earth,
Come hither every year and bring
The boons provocative of mirth;
And should your stock of bass run low,
However much I might repine,
I think I might survive the blow
If plied with wine, and still more wine!

TO JOHN J. KNICKERBOCKER, JR.

Whereas, good friend, it doth appear
You do possess the notion
To his awhile away from here
To lands across the ocean;
Now, by these presents we would show
That, wheresoever wend you,
And wheresoever gales may blow,
Our friendship shall attend you.

What though on Scotia's banks and braes
You pluck the bonnie gowan,
Or chat of old Chicago days
O'er Berlin brew with Cowen;
What though you stroll some boulevard
In Paris (c'est la belle ville!),
Or make the round of Scotland Yard
With our lamented Melville?

Shall paltry leagues of foaming brine
True heart from true hearts sever?
No—in this draught of honest wine
We pledge it, comrade—never!
Though mountain waves between us roll,
Come fortune or disaster—
'Twill knit us closer soul to soul
And bind our friendships faster.

So here's a bowl that shall be quaff'd
To loyalty's devotion,
And here's to fortune that shall waft
Your ship across the ocean,
And here's a smile for those who prate
Of Davy Jones's locker,
And here's a pray'r in every fate—
God bless you, Knickerbocker!

THE BOTTLE AND THE BIRD

Once on a time a friend of mine prevailed on me to go
To see the dazzling splendors of a sinful ballet show,
And after we had reveled in the saltatory sights
We sought a neighboring cafe for more tangible delights;
When I demanded of my friend what viands he preferred,
He quoth: "A large cold bottle and a small hot bird!"

Fool that I was, I did not know what anguish hidden lies
Within the morceau that allures the nostrils and the eyes!
There is a glorious candor in an honest quart of wine—
A certain inspiration which I cannot well define!
How it bubbles, how it sparkles, how its gurgling seems to say:
"Come, on a tide of rapture let me float your soul away!"

But the crispy, steaming mouthful that is spread upon your plate—
How it discounts human sapience and satirizes fate!
You wouldn't think a thing so small could cause the pains and aches
That certainly accrue to him that of that thing partakes;
To me, at least (a guileless wight!) it never once occurred
What horror was encompassed in that one small hot bird.

Oh, what a head I had on me when I awoke next day,
And what a firm conviction of intestinal decay!
What seas of mineral water and of bromide I applied
To quench those fierce volcanic fires that rioted inside!
And, oh! the thousand solemn, awful vows I plighted then
Never to tax my system with a small hot bird again!

The doctor seemed to doubt that birds could worry people so,
But, bless him! since I ate the bird, I guess I ought to know!
The acidous condition of my stomach, so he said,
Bespoke a vinous irritant that amplified my head,
And, ergo, the causation of the thing, as he inferred,
Was the large cold bottle, not the small hot bird.

Of course, I know it wasn't, and I'm sure you'll say I'm right
If ever it has been your wont to train around at night;
How sweet is retrospection when one's heart is bathed in wine,

And before its balmy breath how do the ills of life decline!
How the gracious juices drown what griefs would vex a mortal breast,
And float the flattered soul into the port of dreamless rest!

But you, O noxious, pigmy bird, whether it be you fly
Or paddle in the stagnant pools that sweltering, festering lie—
I curse you and your evil kind for that you do me wrong,
Engendering poisons that corrupt my petted muse of song;
Go, get thee hence, and nevermore discomfit me and mine—
I fain would barter all thy brood for one sweet draught of wine!

So hither come, O sportive youth! when fades the tell-tale day—
Come hither with your fillets and your wreathes of posies gay;
We shall unloose the fragrant seas of seething, frothing wine
Which now the cobwebbed glass and envious wire and corks confine,
And midst the pleasing revelry the praises shall be heard
Of the large cold bottle, not the small hot bird.

THE MAN WHO WORKED WITH DANA ON THE "SUN"

Thar showed up out 'n Denver in the spring of '81
A man who'd worked with Dana on the Noo York Sun.
His name was Cantell Whoppers, 'nd he was a sight ter view
Ez he walked into the orfice 'nd inquired for work to do;
Thar warn't no places vacant then—fer, be it understood,
That was the time when talent flourished at that altitood;
But thar the stranger lingered, tellin' Raymond 'nd the rest
Uv what perdigious wonders he could do when at his best—
'Til finally he stated (quite by chance) that he had done
A heap uv work with Dana on the Noo York Sun.

Wall, that wuz quite another thing; we owned that ary cuss
Who'd worked f'r Mr. Dana must be good enough for us!
And so we tuk the stranger's word 'nd nipped him while we could,
For if we didn't take him we knew John Arkins would—
And Cooper, too, wuz mousin' round for enterprise 'nd brains,
Whenever them commodities blew in across the plains.
At any rate, we nailed him—which made ol' Cooper swear
And Arkins tear out handfuls uv his copious curly hair—
But we set back and cackled, 'nd had a power uv fun
With our man who'd worked with Dana on the Noo York Sun.

It made our eyes hang on our cheeks 'nd lower jaws ter drop
Ter hear that feller tellin' how ol' Dana run his shop;
It seems that Dana was the biggest man you ever saw—
He lived on human bein's 'nd preferred to eat 'em raw!
If he had democratic drugs to take, before he took 'em,
As good old allopathic laws prescribe, he allus shook 'em!
The man that could set down 'nd write like Dana never grew

And the sum of human knowledge wuzn't half what Dana knew.
The consequence appeared to be that nearly everyone
Concurred with Mr. Dana of the Noo York Sun.

This feller, Cantell Whoppers, never brought an item in—
He spent his time at Perrin's shakin' poker dice f'r gin;
Whatever the assignment, he wuz allus sure to shirk—
He wuz very long on likker and all-fired short on work!
If any other cuss had played the tricks he dare ter play,
The daisies would be bloomin' over his remains to-day;
But, somehow, folks respected him and stood him to the last,
Considerin' his superior connections in the past;
So, when he bilked at poker, not a sucker drew a gun
On the man who'd worked with Dana on the Noo York Sun.

Wall, Dana came ter Denver in the fall uv '83—
A very different party from the man we thought ter see!
A nice 'nd clean old gentleman, so dignerfied 'nd calm—
You bet yer life he never did no human bein' harm!
A certain hearty manner 'nd a fullness uv the vest
Betokened that his sperrits 'nd his victuals wuz the best;
His face was so benevolent, his smile so sweet 'nd kind,
That they seemed to be the reflex uv an honest, healthy mind,
And God had set upon his head a crown uv silver hair
In promise of the golden crown He meaneth him to wear;
So, uv us boys that met him out 'n Denver there wuz none
But fell in love with Dana uv the Noo York Sun.

But when he came to Denver in that fall uv '83
His old friend, Cantell Whoppers, disappeared upon a spree;
The very thought uv seein' Dana worked upon him so
(They hadn't been together fer a year or two, you know)
That he borrowed all the stuff he could and started on a bat,
And, strange as it may seem, we didn't see him after that.
So when ol' Dana hove in sight we couldn't understand
Why he didn't seem to notice that his crony wa'n't on hand;
No casual allusion—not a question, no, not one—
For the man who'd "worked with Dana on the Noo York Sun"!

We broke it gently to him, but he didn't seem surprised—
Thar wuz no big burst uv passion as we fellers had surmised;
He said that Whoppers wuz a man he didn't never heerd about,
But he might have carried papers on a Jersey City route—
And then he recollected hearin' Mr. Laflin say
That he fired a man named Whoppers fur bein' drunk one day,
Which, with more likker underneath than money in his vest,
Had started on a freight train fur the great 'nd boundin' West—
But further information or statistics he had none
Uv the man who'd "worked with Dana on the Noo York Sun."

We dropped the matter quietly 'nd never made no fuss—

When we get played fer suckers—why, that's a horse on us!
But every now 'nd then we Denver fellers have to laff
To hear some other paper boast uv havin' on its staff
A man who's "worked with Dana"—'nd then we fellers wink
And pull our hats down on our eyes 'nd set around 'nd think.
It seems like Dana couldn't be as smart as people say
If he educates so many folks 'nd lets 'em get away;
And, as for us, in future we'll be very apt to shun
The man who "worked with Dana on the Noo York Sun"!

But, bless ye, Mr. Dana! may you live a thousan' years,
To sort o' keep things lively in this vale of human tears;
An' may I live a thousan', too—a thousan', less a day,
For I shouldn't like to be on earth to hear you'd passed away.
And when it comes your time to go you'll need no Latin chaff
Nor biographic data put in your epitaph;
But one straight line of English and of truth will let folks know
The homage 'nd the gratitude 'nd reverence they owe;
You'll need no epitaph but this: "Here sleeps the man who run
That best 'nd brightest paper, the Noo York Sun."

A DEMOCRATIC HYMN

Republicans of differing views
Are pro or con protection;
If that's the issue they would choose,
Why, we have no objection.
The issue we propose concerns
Our hearts and homes more nearly:
A wife to whom the nation turns
And venerates so dearly.
So, confident of what shall be,
Our gallant host advances,
Giving three cheers for Grover C.
And three times three for Frances!

So gentle is that honored dame,
And fair beyond all telling,
The very mention of her name
Sets every breast to swelling.
She wears no mortal crown of gold—
No courtiers fawn around her—
But with their love young hearts and old
In loyalty have crowned her—
And so with Grover and his bride
We're proud to take our chances,
And it's three times three for the twain give we—
But particularly for Frances!

The Blue and the Gray collided one day
In the future great town of Missouri,
And if all that we hear is the truth, 'twould appear
That they tackled each other with fury.

While the weather waxed hot they hove and they sot,
Like the scow in the famous old story,
And what made the fight an enjoyable sight
Was the fact that they fought con amore.

They as participants fought in such wise as was taught,
As beseemed the old days of the dragons,
When you led to the dance and defended with lance
The damsel you pledged in your flagons.

In their dialect way the knights of the Gray
Gave a flout at the buckeye bandana,
And the buckeye came back with a gosh-awful whack,
And that's what's the matter with Hannah.

This resisted attack took the Grays all a-back,
And feeling less coltish and frisky,
They resolved to elate the cause of their state,
And also their persons, with whisky.

Having made ample use of the treacherous juice,
Which some folks say stings like an adder,
They went back again at the handkerchief men,
Who slowly got madder and madder.

You can bet it was h—l in the Southern Hotel
And elsewhere, too many to mention,
But the worst of it all was achieved in the hall
Where the President held his convention.

They ripped and they hewed and they, sweating imbrued,
Volleyed and bellowed and thundered;
There was nothing to do until these yawpers got through,
So the rest of us waited and wondered.

As the result of these frays it appears that the Grays,
Who once were as chipper as daisies,
Have changed their complexion to one of dejection,
And at present are bluer than blazes.

IT IS THE PRINTER'S FAULT

In Mrs. Potter's latest play
The costuming is fine;
Her waist is made decollete—
Her skirt is new design.

SUMMER HEAT

Nay, why discuss this summer heat,
Of which vain people tell?
Oh, sinner, rather were it meet
To fix thy thoughts on hell!

The punishment ordained for you
In that infernal spot
Is het by Satan's impish crew
And kept forever hot.

Sumatra might be reckoned nice,
And Tophet passing cool,
And Sodom were a cake of ice
Beside that sulphur pool.

An awful stench and dismal wail
Come from the broiling souls,
Whilst Satan with his fireproof tail
Stirs up the brimstone coals.

Oh, sinner, on this end 'tis meet
That thou shouldst ponder well,
For what, oh, what, is worldly heat
Unto the heat of hell?

PLAINT OF THE MISSOURI 'COON IN THE BERLIN ZOOLOGICAL GARDENS

Friend, by the way you hump yourself you're from the States, I know,
And born in old Mizzourah, where the 'coons in plenty grow;
I, too, am a native of that clime, but harsh, relentless fate
Has doomed me to an exile far from that noble state,
And I, who used to climb around and swing from tree to tree,
Now lead a life of ignominious ease, as you can see.
Have pity, O compatriot mine! and bide a season near
While I unfurl a dismal tale to catch your friendly ear.

My pedigree is noble—they used my grandsire's skin
To piece a coat for Patterson to warm himself within—

Tom Patterson of Denver; no ermine can compare
With the grizzled robe that democratic statesman loves to wear!
Of such a grandsire I have come, and in the County Cole,
All up an ancient cottonwood, our family had its hole—
We envied not the liveried pomp nor proud estate of kings
As we hustled around from day to day in search of bugs and things.

And when the darkness fell around, a mocking bird was nigh,
Inviting pleasant, soothing dreams with his sweet lullaby;
And sometimes came the yellow dog to brag around all night
That nary 'coon could wollop him in a stand-up barrel fight;
We simply smiled and let him howl, for all Mizzourians know
That ary 'coon can beat a dog if the 'coon gets half a show!
But we'd nestle close and shiver when the mellow moon had ris'n
And the hungry nigger sought our lair in hopes to make us his'n!

Raised as I was, it's hardly strange I pine for those old days—
I cannot get acclimated or used to German ways;
The victuals that they give me here may all be very fine
For vulgar, common palates, but they will not do for mine!
The 'coon that's been used to stanch democratic cheer
Will not put up with onion tarts and sausage steeped in beer!
No; let the rest, for meat and drink, accede to slavish terms,
But send me back from whence I came and let me grub for worms!

They come (these gaping Teutons do) on Sunday afternoons
And wonder what I am—alas! there are no German 'coons!
For, if there were, I might still swing at home from tree to tree,
A symbol of democracy that's woolly, blythe and free.
And yet for what my captors are I would not change my lot,
For I have tasted liberty—these others, they have not!
So, even caged, the democratic 'coon more glory feels
Than the conscript German puppets with their swords about their heels!

Well, give my love to Crittenden, to Clardy and O'Neill,
To Jasper Burke and Colonel Jones, and tell 'em how I feel;
My compliments to Cockrill, Munford, Switzler, Hasbrook, Vest,
Bill Nelson, J. West Goodwin, Jedge Broadhead and the rest;
Bid them be steadfast in the faith and pay no heed at all
To Joe McCullagh's badinage or Chauncy Filley's gall;
And urge them to retaliate for what I'm suffering here
By cinching all the alien class that wants its Sunday beer.

THE BIBLIOMANIAC'S BRIDE

The women folk are like to books—
Most pleasing to the eye,
Whereon if anybody looks
He feels disposed to buy.

I hear that many are for sale—
Those that record no dates,
And such editions as regale
The view with colored plates.

Of every quality and grade
And size they may be found—
Quite often beautifully made,
As often poorly bound.

Now, as for me, had I my choice,
I'd choose no folio tall,
But some octavo to rejoice
My sight and heart withal.

As plump and pudgy as a snipe—
Well worth her weight in gold,
Of honest, clean, conspicuous type,
And just the size to hold!

With such a volume for my wife,
How should I keep and con?
How like a dream should speed my life
Unto its colophon!

Her frontispiece should be more fair
Than any colored plate;
Blooming with health she would not care
To extra-illustrate.

And in her pages there should be
A wealth of prose and verse,
With now and then a jeu d'esprit—
But nothing ever worse!

Prose for me when I wished for prose,
Verse, when to verse inclined—
Forever bringing sweet repose
To body, heart, and mind.

Oh, I should bind this priceless prize
In bindings full and fine,
And keep her where no human eyes
Should see her charms, but mine!

With such a fair unique as this,
What happiness abounds!
Who—who could paint my rapturous bliss,
My joy unknown to Lowndes!

EZRA J. M'MANUS TO A SOUBRETTE

'Tis years, soubrette, since last we met,
And yet, ah yet, how swift and tender
My thoughts go back in Time's dull track
To you, sweet pink of female gender!
I shall not say—though others may—
That time all human joy enhances;
But the same old thrill comes to me still
With memories of your songs and dances.

Soubrettish ways these latter days
Invite my praise, but never get it;
I still am true to yours and you—
My record's made—I'll not upset it!
The pranks they play, the things they say—
I'd blush to put the like on paper;
And I'll avow they don't know how
To dance, so awkwardly they caper!

I used to sit down in the pit
And see you flit like elf or fairy
Across the stage, and I'll engage
No moonbeam sprite were half so airy.
Lo! everywhere about me there
Were rivals reeking with pomatum,
And if perchance they caught a glance
In song or dance, how did I hate 'em!

At half-past ten came rapture—then
Of all those men was I most happy,
For wine and things and food for kings
And tete-a-tetes were on the tapis.
Did you forget, my fair soubrette,
Those suppers in the Cafe Rector—
The cozy nook where we partook
Of sweeter draughts than fabled nectar?

Oh, happy days, when youth's wild ways
Knew every phase of harmless folly!
Oh, blissful nights whose fierce delights
Defied gaunt-featured Melancholy!
Gone are they all beyond recall,
And I, a shade—a mere reflection—
Am forced to feed my spirits' greed
Upon the husks of retrospection.

And lo! to-night the phantom light
That as a sprite flits on the fender

Reveals a face whose girlish grace
Brings back the feeling, warm and tender;
And all the while the old time smile
Plays on my visage, grim and wrinkled,
As though, soubrette, your footfalls yet
Upon my rusty heart-strings tinkled.

THE MONSTROUS PLEASANT BALLAD OF THE TAYLOR PUP

Now lithe and listen, gentles all,
Now lithe ye all and hark
Unto a ballad I shall sing
About Buena Park.

Of all the wonders happening there
The strangest hap befell
Upon a famous April morn,
As you I now shall tell.

It is about the Taylor pup
And of his mistress eke,
And of the pranking time they had
That I would fain to speak.

FITTE THE FIRST

The pup was of a noble mein
As e'er you gazed upon;
They called his mother Lady
And his father was a Don.

And both his mother and his sire
Were of the race Bernard—
The family famed in histories
And hymned of every bard.

His form was of exuberant mold,
Long, slim and loose of joints;
There never was a pointer-dog
So full as he of points.

His hair was like a yellow fleece,
His eyes were black and kind,
And like a nodding, gilded plume
His tail stuck up behind.

His bark was very, very fierce
And fierce his appetite,

Yet was it only things to eat
That he was prone to bite.

But in that one particular
He was so passing true
That never did he quit a meal
Until he had got through.

Potatoes, biscuits, mush or hash,
Joint, chop, or chicken limb—
So long as it was edible,
'Twas all the same to him!

And frequently when Hunger's pangs
Assailed that callow pup,
He masticated boots and gloves
Or chewed a door-mat up.

So was he much beholden of
The folk that him did keep;
They loved him when he was awake
And better still asleep.

FITTE THE SECOND

Now once his master lingering o'er
His breakfast coffee-cup,
Observed unto his doting spouse:
"You ought to wash the pup!"

"That shall I do this very day,"
His doting spouse replied;
"You will not know the pretty thing
When he is washed and dried.

"But tell me, dear, before you go
Unto your daily work,
Shall I use Ivory soap on him,
Or Colgate, Pears' or Kirk?"

"Odzooks, it matters not a whit—
They all are good to use!
Take Pearline, if it pleases you—
Sapolio, if you choose!

"Take any soap, but take the pup
And also water take,
And mix the three discreetly up
Till they a lather make.

"Then mixing these constituent parts,
Let nature take her way,"
With such advice that sapient sir
Had nothing more to say.

Then fared he to his daily toil
All in the Board of Trade,
While Mistress Taylor for that bath
Due preparations made.

FITTE THE THIRD

She whistled gayly to the pup
And called him by his name,
And presently the guileless thing
All unsuspecting came.

But when she shut the bath-room door
And caught him as catch-can,
And dove him in that odious tub,
His sorrows then began.

How did that callow, yellow thing
Regret that April morn—
Alas! how bitterly he rued
The day that he was born!

Twice and again, but all in vain
He lifted up his wail;
His voice was all the pup could lift,
For thereby hangs this tale.

'Twas by that tail she held him down
And presently she spread
The creamery lather on his back,
His stomach and his head.

His ears hung down in sorry wise,
His eyes were, oh! so sad—
He looked as though he just had lost
The only friend he had.

And higher yet the water rose,
The lather still increased,
And sadder still the countenance
Of that poor martyred beast!

Yet all this time his mistress spoke
Such artful words of cheer
As "Oh, how nice!" and "Oh, how clean!"

And "There's a patient dear!"

At last the trial had an end,
At last the pup was free;
She threw awide the bath-room door—
"Now get you gone!" quoth she.

FITTE THE FOURTH

Then from that tub and from that room
He gat with vast ado;
At every hop he gave a shake
And—how the water flew!

He paddled down the winding stairs
And to the parlor hied,
Dispensing pools of foamy suds
And slop on every side.

Upon the carpet then he rolled
And brushed against the wall,
And, horror! whisked his lathery sides
On overcoat and shawl.

Attracted by the dreadful din,
His mistress came below—
Who, who can speak her wonderment—
Who, who can paint her woe!

Great smears of soap were here and there—
Her startled vision met
With blots of lather everywhere,
And everything was wet!

Then Mrs. Taylor gave a shriek
Like one about to die;
"Get out—get out, and don't you dare
Come in till you are dry!"

With that she opened wide the door
And waved the critter through;
Out in the circumambient air
With grateful yelp he flew.

FITTE THE FIFTH

He whisked into the dusty street
And to the Waller lot
Where bonny Annie Evans played

With charming Sissy Knott.

And with these pretty little dears
He mixed himself all up—
Oh, fie upon such boisterous play—
Fie, fie, you naughty pup!

Woe, woe on Annie's India mull,
And Sissy's blue percale!
One got the pup's belathered flanks,
And one his soapy tail!

Forth to the rescue of those maids
Rushed gallant Willie Clow;
His panties they were white and clean—
Where are those panties now?

Where is the nicely laundered shirt
That Kendall Evans wore,
And Robbie James' tricot coat
All buttoned up before?

The leaven, which, as we are told,
Leavens a monstrous lump,
Hath far less reaching qualities
Than a wet pup on the jump.

This way and that he swung and swayed,
He gamboled far and near,
And everywhere he thrust himself
He left a soapy smear.

FITTE THE SIXTH

That noon a dozen little dears
Were spanked and put to bed
With naught to stay their appetites
But cheerless crusts of bread.

That noon a dozen hired girls
Washed out each gown and shirt
Which that exuberant Taylor pup
Had frescoed o'er with dirt.

That whole day long the April sun
Smiled sweetly from above
On clothes lines flaunting to the breeze
With emblems mothers love.

That whole day long the Taylor pup

This way and that did hie
Upon his mad, erratic course
Intent on getting dry.

That night when Mr. Taylor came
His vesper meal to eat,
He uttered things my pious pen
Would liefer not repeat.

Yet still that noble Taylor pup
Survives to romp and bark
And stumble over folks and things
In fair Buena Park.

Good sooth, I wot he should be called
Buena's favorite son
Who's sired of such a noble sire
And damned by every one.

LONG METER

All human joys are swift of wing
For heaven doth so allot it
That when you get an easy thing
You find you haven't got it.

Man never yet has loved a maid,
But they were sure to part, sir;
Nor never lacked a paltry spade
But that he drew a heart, sir!

Go, Chauncey! it is plain as day
You much prefer a dinner
To walking straight in wisdom's way—
Go to, thou babbling sinner.

The froward part that you have played
To me this lesson teaches:
To trust no man whose stock in trade
Is after-dinner speeches.

TO DE WITT MILLER

Dear Miller: You and I despise
The cad who gathers books to sell 'em,
Be they but sixteen-mos in cloth
Or stately folios garbed in vellum.

But when one fellow has a prize
Another bibliophile is needing,
Why, then, a satisfactory trade
Is quite a laudable proceeding.

There's precedent in Bristol's case
The great collector—preacher-farmer;
And in the case of that divine
Who shrives the soul of P.D. Armour.

When from their sapient, saintly lips
The words of wisdom are not dropping,
They turn to trade—that is to say,
When they're not preaching they are swapping!

So to the flock it doth appear
That this a most conspicuous fact is:
That which these godly pastors do
Must surely be a proper practice.

Now, here's a pretty prize, indeed,
On which De Vinne's art is lavished;
Harkee! the bonny, dainty thing
Is simply waiting to be ravished!

And you have that for which I pine
As you should pine for this fair creature:
Come, now, suppose we make a trade—
You take this gem, and send the Beecher!

Surely, these graceful, tender songs
(In samite garb with lots of gilt on)
Are more to you than those dull tome?
Her pastor gave to Lizzie Tilton!

FRANCOIS VILLON

If I were Francois Villon and Francois Villon I,
What would it matter to me how the time might drag or fly?
He would in sweaty anguish toil the days and night away,
And still not keep the prowling, growling, howling wolf at bay!
But, with my valiant bottle and my frouzy brevet-bride,
And my score of loyal cut-throats standing guard for me outside,
What worry of the morrow would provoke a casual sigh
If I were Francois Villon and Francois Villon I?

If I were Francois Villon and Francois Villon I,
To yonder gloomy boulevard at midnight I would hie;

"Stop, stranger! and deliver your possessions, ere you feel
The mettle of my bludgeon or the temper of my steel!"
He should give me gold and diamonds, his snuffbox and his cane—
"Now back, my boon companions, to our brothel with our gain!"
And, back within that brothel, how the bottles they would fly,
If I were Francois Villon and Francois Villon I!

If I were Francois Villon and Francois Villon I,
We both would mock the gibbet which the law has lifted high;
He in his meager, shabby home, I in my roaring den—
He with his babes around him, I with my hunted men!
His virtue be his bulwark—my genius should be mine!—
"Go fetch my pen, sweet Margot, and a jorum of your wine!"

So would one vainly plod, and one win immortality—
If I were Francois Villon and Francois Villon I!

LYDIA DICK

When I was a boy at college,
Filling up with classic knowledge,
Frequently I wondered why
Old Professor Demas Bently
Used to praise so eloquently
"Opera Horatii."

Toiling on a season longer
Till my reasoning power got stronger,
As my observation grew,
I became convinced that mellow,
Massic-loving poet fellow
Horace knew a thing or two

Yes, we sophomores figured duly
That, if we appraised him truly,
Horace must have been a brick;
And no wonder that with ranting
Rhymes he went a-gallivanting
Round with sprightly Lydia Dick!

For that pink of female gender
Tall and shapely was, and slender,
Plump of neck and bust and arms;
While the raiment that invested
Her so jealously suggested
Certain more potential charms.

Those dark eyes of her that fired him—
Those sweet accents that inspired him,

And her crown of glorious hair—
These things baffle my description;
I should have a fit conniption
If I tried—so I forbear!

May be Lydia had her betters;
Anyway, this man of letters
Took that charmer as his pick;
Glad—yes, glad I am to know it!
I, a fin de siecle poet,
Sympathize with Lydia Dick!

Often in my arbor shady
I fall thinking of that lady
And the pranks she used to play;
And I'm cheered—for all we sages
Joy when from those distant ages
Lydia dances down our way.

Otherwise some folks might wonder
With good reason why in thunder
Learned professors, dry and prim,
Find such solace in the giddy
Pranks that Horace played with Liddy
Or that Liddy played on him.

Still this world of ours rejoices
In those ancient singing voices,
And our hearts beat high and quick,
To the cadence of old Tiber
Murmuring praise of roistering Liber
And of charming Lydia Dick.

Still, Digentia, downward flowing,
Prattleth to the roses blowing
By the dark, deserted grot;
Still, Soracte, looming lonely,
Watcheth for the coming only
Of a ghost that cometh not.

THE TIN BANK

Speaking of banks, I'm bound to say
That a bank of tin is far the best,
And I know of one that has stood for years
In a pleasant home away out west.
It has stood for years on the mantelpiece
Between the clock and the Wedgwood plate—
A wonderful bank, as you'll concede

When you've heard the things I'll now relate.

This bank was made of McKinley tin,
Well soldered up at sides and back;
But it didn't resemble tin at all,
For they'd painted it over an iron black.
And that it really was a bank
'Twas an easy thing to see and say,
For above the door in gorgeous red
Appeared the letters B-A-N-K!

The bank had been so well devised
And wrought so cunningly that when
You put your money in at the hole
It couldn't get out of that hole again!
Somewhere about that stanch, snug thing
A secret spring was hid away,
But where it was or how it worked—
Excuse me, please, but I will not say.

Thither, with dimpled cheeks aglow,
Came pretty children oftentimes,
And, standing up on stool or chair,
Put in their divers pence and dimes.
Once Uncle Hank came home from town
After a cycle of grand events,
And put in a round, blue, ivory thing,
He said was good for 50 cents!

The bank went clinkety-clinkety-clink,
And larger grew the precious sum
Which grandma said she hoped would prove
A gracious boon to heathendom!
But there were those—I call no names—
Who did not fancy any plan
That did not in some wise involve
The candy and banana man.

Listen; once when the wind went "Yooooooo!"
And the raven croaked in the tangled tarn—
When, with a wail, the screech-owl flew
Out of her lair in the haunted barn—
There came three burglars down the road—
Three burglars skilled in arts of sin,
And they cried: "What's this? Aha! Oho!"
And straightway tackled the bank of tin.

They burgled from half-past ten p.m.,
Till the village bell struck four o'clock;
They hunted and searched and guessed and tried—
But the little tin bank would not unlock!

They couldn't discover the secret spring!
So, when the barn-yard rooster crowed,
They up with their tools and stole away
With the bitter remark that they'd be blowed!

Next morning came a sweet-faced child
And reached her dimpled hand to take
A nickel to send to the heathen poor
And a nickel to spend for her stomach's sake.
She pressed the hidden secret spring,
And lo! the bank flew open then
With a cheery creak that seemed to say:
"I'm glad to see you; come again!"

If you were I, and if I were you,
What would we keep our money in?
In a downtown bank of British steel,
Or an at-home bank of McKinley tin?
Some want silver and some want gold,
But the little tin bank that wants the two
And is run on the double standard plan—
Why, that is the bank for me and you!

IN NEW ORLEANS

'Twas in the Crescent city not long ago befell
The tear-compelling incident I now propose to tell;
So come, my sweet collector friends, and listen while I sing
Unto your delectation this brief, pathetic thing—
No lyric pitched in vaunting key, but just a requiem
Of blowing twenty dollars in by 9 o'clock a.m.

Let critic folk the poet's use of vulgar slang upbraid,
But, when I'm speaking by the card, I call a spade a spade;
And I, who have been touched of that same mania, myself,
Am well aware that, when it comes to parting with his pelf,
The curio collector is so blindly lost in sin
That he doesn't spend his money—he simply blows it in!

In Royal Street (near Conti) there's a lovely curio-shop,
And there, one balmy, fateful morn, it was my chance to stop:
To stop was hesitation—in a moment I was lost—
That kind of hesitation does not hesitate at cost:
I spied a pewter tankard there, and, my! it was a gem—
And the clock in old St. Louis told the hour of 8 a.m.!

Three quaint Bohemian bottles, too, of yellow and of green,
Cut in archaic fashion that I ne'er before had seen;
A lovely, hideous platter wreathed about with pink and rose,

With its curious depression into which the gravy flows;
Two dainty silver salters—oh, there was no resisting them.—
And I'd blown in twenty dollars by 9 o'clock a.m.

With twenty dollars, one who is a prudent man, indeed,
Can buy the wealth of useful things his wife and children need;
Shoes, stockings, knickerbockers, gloves, bibs, nursing-bottles, caps,
A gown—the gown for which his spouse too long has pined, perhaps!
These and ten thousand other specters harrow and condemn
The man who's blowing in twenty by 9 o'clock a.m.

Oh, mean advantage conscience takes (and one that I abhor!)
In asking one this question: "What did you buy it for?"
Why doesn't conscience ply its blessed trade before the act,
Before one's cussedness becomes a bald, accomplished fact—
Before one's fallen victim to the Tempter's strategem
And blown in twenty dollars by 9 o'clock a.m.?

Ah, me! now the deed is done, how penitent I am!
I was a roaring lion—behold a bleating lamb!
I've packed and shipped those precious things to that most precious wife
Who shares with our sweet babes the strange vicissitudes of life,
While he, who, in his folly, gave up his store of wealth,
Is far away, and means to keep his distance—for his health!

THE PETER-BIRD

Out of the woods by the creek cometh a calling for Peter,
From the orchard a voice echoes and echoes it over;
Down in the pasture the sheep hear that strange crying for Peter,
Over the meadows that call is aye and forever repeated.
So let me tell you the tale, when, where and how it all happened,
And, when the story is told, let us pay heed to the lesson.

Once on a time, long ago, lived in the state of Kentucky
One that was reckoned a witch—full of strange spells and devices;
Nightly she wandered the woods, searching for charms voodooistic—
Scorpions, lizards, and herbs, dormice, chameleons and plantains!
Serpents and caw-caws and bats, screech-owls and crickets and adders—
These were the guides of the witch through the dank deeps of the forest.
Then, with her roots and her herbs, back to her cave in the morning
Ambled that hussy to brew spells of unspeakable evil;
And, when the people awoke, seeing the hillside and valley
Sweltered in swathes as of mist—"Look!" they would whisper in terror—
"Look! the old witch is at work brewing her spells of great evil!"
Then would they pray till the sun, darting his rays through the vapor,
Lifted the smoke from the earth and baffled the witch's intentions.

One of the boys at that time was a certain young person named Peter,

Given too little to work, given too largely to dreaming;
Fonder of books than of chores you can imagine that Peter
Led a sad life on the farm, causing his parents much trouble.
"Peter!" his mother would call, "the cream is a-ready for churning!"
"Peter!" his father would cry, "go grub at the weeds in the garden!"
So it was "Peter!" all day—calling, reminding and chiding—
Peter neglected his work; therefore that nagging at Peter!

Peter got hold of some books—how I'm unable to tell you;
Some have suspected the witch—this is no place for suspicions!
It is sufficient to stick close to the thread of the legend.
Nor is it stated or guessed what was the trend of those volumes;
What thing soever it was—done with a pen and a pencil,
Wrought with the brain, not a hoe—surely 'twas hostile to farming!
"Fudge on the readin'!" they quoth; "that's what's the ruin of Peter!"

So, when the mornings were hot, under the beech or the maple,
Cushioned in grass that was blue, breathing the breath of the blossoms.
Lulled by the hum of the bees, the coo of the ringdoves a-mating,
Peter would frivol his time at reading, or lazing, or dreaming.
"Peter!" his mother would call, "the cream is a-ready for churning!"
"Peter!" his father would cry, "go grub at the weeds in the garden!"
"Peter!" and "Peter!" all day—calling, reminding and chiding—
Peter neglected his chores; therefore that outcry for Peter;
Therefore the neighbors allowed evil would surely befall him—
Yes, on account of these things, ruin would come upon Peter!

Surely enough, on a time, reading and lazing and dreaming
Wrought the calamitous ill all had predicted for Peter;
For, of a morning in spring when lay the mist in the valleys—
"See," quoth the folk, "how the witch breweth her evil decoctions!
See how the smoke from her fire broodeth on wood land and meadow!
Grant that the sun cometh out to smother the smudge of her caldron!
She hath been forth in the night, full of her spells and devices,
Roaming the marshes and dells for heathenish musical nostrums;
Digging in leaves and at stumps for centipedes, pismires and spiders,
Grubbing in poisonous pools for hot salmanders and toadstools;
Charming the bats from the flues, snaring the lizards by twilight,
Sucking the scorpion's egg and milking the breast of the adder!"

Peter derided these things held in such faith by the farmer,
Scouted at magic and charms, hooted at Jonahs and hoodoos—
Thinking the reading of books must have unsettled his reason!
"There ain't no witches," he cried; "it isn't smoky, but foggy!
I will go out in the wet—you all can't hender me, nuther!"

Surely enough he went out into the damp of the morning,
Into the smudge that the witch spread over woodland and meadow,
Into the fleecy gray pall brooding on hillside and valley.
Laughing and scoffing, he strode into that hideous vapor;
Just as he said he would do, just as he bantered and threatened,

Ere they could fasten the door, Peter had gone and done it!
Wasting his time over books, you see, had unsettled his reason—
Soddened his callow young brain with semi-pubescent paresis,
And his neglect of his chores hastened this evil condition.

Out of the woods by the creek cometh a calling for Peter
And from the orchard a voice echoes and echoes it over;
Down in the pasture the sheep hear that shrill crying for Peter,
Up from the spring-house the wail stealeth anon like a whisper,
Over the meadows that call is aye and forever repeated.
Such are the voices that whooped wildly and vainly for Peter
Decades and decades ago down in the state of Kentucky—
Such are the voices that cry from the woodland and meadow,
"Peter—O Peter!" all day, calling, reminding, and chiding—
Taking us back to the time when Peter he done gone and done it!
These are the voices of those left by the boy in the farmhouse
When, with his laughter and scorn, hatless and bootless and sockless,
Clothed in his jeans and his pride, Peter sailed out in the weather,
Broke from the warmth of his home into that fog of the devil.
Into the smoke of that witch brewing her damnable porridge!

Lo, when he vanished from sight, knowing the evil that threatened,
Forth with importunate cries hastened his father and mother.
"Peter!" they shrieked in alarm, "Peter!" and evermore "Peter!"—
Ran from the house to the barn, ran from the barn to the garden,
Ran to the corn-crib anon, then to the smokehouse proceeded;
Henhouse and woodpile they passed, calling and wailing and weeping,
Through the front gate to the road, braving the hideous vapor—
Sought him in lane and on pike, called him in orchard and meadow,
Clamoring "Peter!" in vain, vainly outcrying for Peter.
Joining the search came the rest, brothers, and sisters and cousins,
Venting unspeakable fears in pitiful wailing for Peter!
And from the neighboring farms gathered the men and the women.
Who, upon hearing the news, swelled the loud chorus for Peter.

Farmers and hussifs and maids, bosses and field-hands and niggers,
Colonels and jedges galore from corn-fields and mint-beds and thickets.
All that had voices to voice, all to those parts appertaining.
Came to engage in the search, gathered and bellowed for Peter.
The Taylors, the Dorseys, the Browns, the Wallers, the Mitchells, the Logans.
The Yenowines, Crittendens, Dukes, the Hickmans, the Hobbses, the Morgans;
The Ormsbys, the Thompsons, the Hikes, the Williamsons, Murrays and Hardins,
The Beynroths, the Sherlays, the Hokes, the Haldermans, Harneys and Slaughters—
All famed in Kentucky of old for prowess prodigious at farming.
Now surged from their prosperous homes to join in the hunt for the truant.
To ascertain where he was at, to help out the chorus for Peter.

Still on these prosperous farms were heirs and assigns of the people
Specified hereinabove and proved by the records of probate—
Still on these farms shall you hear (and still on the turnpikes adjacent)
That pitiful, petulant call, that pleading, expostulant wailing,

That hopeless, monotonous moan, that crooning and droning for Peter.
Some say the witch in her wrath transmogrified all those good people;
That, wakened from slumber that day by the calling and bawling for Peter,
She out of her cave in a trice, and, waving the foot of a rabbit
(Crossed with the caul of a coon and smeared with the blood of a chicken),
She changed all these folks into birds and shrieking with demoniac venom:
"Fly away over the land, moaning your Peter forever,
Croaking of Peter, the boy who didn't believe there were hoodoos,
Crooning of Peter the fool who scouted at stories of witches.
Crying for Peter for aye, forever outcalling for Peter!"

This is the story they tell; so in good sooth saith the legend:
As I have told, so tell the folk and the legend,
That it is true I believe, for on the breeze of the morning
Come the shrill voices of birds calling and calling for Peter;
Out of the maple and beech glitter the eyes of the wailers,
Peeping and peering for him who formerly lived in these places—
Peter, the heretic lad, lazy and careless and dreaming,
Sorely afflicted with books and with pubescent paresis.
Hating the things of the farm, care of the barn and the garden.
Always neglecting his chores—given to books and to reading,
Which, as all people allow, turn the young person to mischief,
Harden his heart against toil, wean his affections from tillage.

This is the legend of yore told in the state of Kentucky
When in the springtime the birds call from the beeches and maples,
Call from the petulant thorn, call from the acrid persimmon;
When from the woods by the creek and from the pastures and meadows,
When from the spring-house and lane and from the mint-bed and orchard,
When from the redbud and gum and from redolent lilac,
When from the dirt roads and pikes comes that calling for Peter;
Cometh the dolorous cry, cometh that weird iteration
Of "Peter" and "Peter" for aye, of "Peter" and "Peter" forever!
This is the legend of old, told in the tumtitty meter
Which the great poets prefer, being less labor than rhyming
(My first attempt at the same, my last attempt, too, I reckon,)
Nor have I further to say, for the sad story is ended.

DIBDIN'S GHOST

Dear wife, last midnight while I read
The tomes you so despise,
A specter rose beside the bed
And spoke in this true wise;
"From Canaan's beatific coast
I've come to visit thee,
For I'm Frognall Dibdin's ghost!"
Says Dibdin's ghost to me.

I bade him welcome and we twain
Discussed with buoyant hearts
The various things that appertain
To bibliomaniac arts.
"Since you are fresh from t'other side,
Pray tell me of that host
That treasured books before they died,"
Says I to Dibdin's ghost.

"They've entered into perfect rest,
For in the life they've won
There are no auctions to molest,
No creditors to dun;
Their heavenly rapture has no bounds
Beside that jasper sea—
It is a joy unknown to Lowndes!"
Says Dibdin's ghost to me.

Much I rejoiced to hear him speak
Of biblio-bliss above,
For I am one of those who seek
What bibliomaniacs love;
"But tell me—for I long to hear
What doth concern me most—
Are wives admitted to that sphere?"
Says I to Dibdin's ghost.

"The women folk are few up there,
For 'twere not fair you know
That they our heavenly joy should share
Who vex us here below!
The few are those who have been kind
To husbands such as we—
They knew our fads, and didn't mind,"
Says Dibdin's ghost to me.

"But what of those who scold at us
When we would read in bed?
Or, wanting victuals, make a fuss
If we buy books, instead?
And what of those who've dusted not
Our motley pride and boast?
Shall they profane that sacred spot?"
Says I to Dibdin's ghost.

"Oh, no! they tread that other path
Which leads where torments roll,
And worms—yes bookworms—vent their wrath
Upon the guilty soul!
Untouched of bibliomaniac grace
That saveth such as we,

They wallow in that dreadful place!"
Says Dibdin's ghost to me.

"To my dear wife will I recite
What things I've heard you say;
She'll let me read the books by night
She's let me buy by day;
For we, together, by and by,
Would join that heavenly host—
She's earned a rest as well as I!"
Says I to Dibdin's ghost.

AN AUTUMN TREASURE-TROVE

'Tis the time of the year's sundown, and flame
Hangs on the maple bough;
And June is the faded flower of a name;
The thin hedge hides not a singer now.
Yet rich am I; for my treasures be
The gold afloat in my willow-tree.

Sweet morn on the hillside dripping with dew,
Girded with blue and pearl,
Counts the leaves afloat in the streamlet too;
As the love-lorn heart of a wistful girl,
She sings while her soul brooding tearfully
Sees a dream of gold in the willow-tree.

All day pure white and saffron at eve,
Clouds awaiting the sun
Turn them at length to ghosts that leave
When the moon's white path is slowly run
Till the morning comes, and with joy for me
O'er my gold agleam in the willow-tree.

The lilacs that blew on the breast of May
Are an old and lost delight;
And the rose lies ruined in his careless way
As the wind turns the poplars underwhite,
Yet richer am I for the autumn; see
All my misty gold in the willow-tree.

WHEN THE POET CAME

The ferny places gleam at morn,
The dew drips off the leaves of corn;
Along the brook a mist of white

Fades as a kiss on lips of light;
For, lo! the poet with his pipe
Finds all these melodies are ripe!

Far up within the cadenced June
Floats, silver-winged, a living tune
That winds within the morning's chime
And sets the earth and sky to rhyme;
For, lo! the poet, absent long,
Breathes the first raptures of his song!

Across the clover-blossoms, wet,
With dainty clumps of violet,
And wild red roses in her hair,
There comes a little maiden fair.
I cannot more of June rehearse—
She is the ending of my verse.

Ah, nay! For through perpetual days
Of summer gold and filmy haze,
When Autumn dies in Winter's sleet,
I yet will see those dew-washed feet,
And o'er the tracts of Life and Time
They make the cadence for my rhyme.

THE PERPETUAL WOOING

The dull world clamors at my feet
And asks my hand and helping sweet;
And wonders when the time shall be
I'll leave off dreaming dreams of thee.
It blames me coining soul and time
And sending minted bits of rhyme—
A-wooing of thee still.

Shall I make answer? This it is:
I camp beneath thy galaxies
Of starry thoughts and shining deeds;
And, seeing new ones, I must needs
Arouse my speech to tell thee, dear,
Though thou art nearer, I am near—
A-wooing of thee still.

I feel thy heart-beat next mine own;
Its music hath a richer tone.
I rediscover in thine eyes
A balmier, dewier paradise.
I'm sure thou art a rarer girl—
And so I seek thee, finest pearl,

A-wooing of thee still.

With blood of roses on thy lips—
Canst doubt my trembling?—something slips
Between thy loveliness and me—
So commonplace, so fond of thee.
Ah, sweet, a kiss is waiting where
That last one stopped thy lover's prayer—
A-wooing of thee still.

When new light falls upon thy face
My gladdened soul discerns some trace
Of God, or angel, never seen
In other days of shade and sheen.
Ne'er may such rapture die, or less
Than joy like this my heart confess—
A-wooing of thee still.

Go thou, O soul of beauty, go
Fleet-footed toward the heavens aglow.
Mayhap, in following, thou shalt see
Me worthier of thy love and thee.
Thou wouldst not have me satisfied
Until thou lov'st me—none beside—
A-wooing of thee still.

This was a song of years ago—
Of spring! Now drifting flowers of snow
Bloom on the window-sills as white
As gray-beard looking through love's light
And holding blue-veined hands the while.
He finds her last—the sweetest smile—
A-wooing of her still.

MY PLAYMATES

The wind comes whispering to me of the country green and cool—
Of redwing blackbirds chattering beside a reedy pool;
It brings me soothing fancies of the homestead on the hill,
And I hear the thrush's evening song and the robin's morning trill;
So I fall to thinking tenderly of those I used to know
Where the sassafras and snakeroot and checker-berries grow.

What has become of Ezra Marsh who lived on Baker's hill?
And what's become of Noble Pratt whose father kept the mill?
And what's become of Lizzie Crum and Anastasia Snell,
And of Roxie Root who 'tended school in Boston for a spell?
They were the boys and they the girls who shared my youthful play—
They do not answer to my call! My playmates—where are they?

What has become of Levi and his little brother Joe
Who lived next door to where we lived some forty years ago?
I'd like to see the Newton boys and Quincy Adams Brown,
And Hepsy Hall and Ella Cowles who spelled the whole school down!
And Gracie Smith, the Cutler boys, Leander Snow and all
Who I'm sure would answer could they only hear my call!

I'd like to see Bill Warner and the Conkey boys again
And talk about the times we used to wish that we were men!
And one—I shall not name her—could I see her gentle face
And hear her girlish treble in this distant, lonely place!
The flowers and hopes of springtime—they perished long ago
And the garden where they blossomed is white with winter snow.

O cottage 'neath the maples, have you seen those girls and boys
That but a little while ago made, oh! such pleasant noise?
O trees, and hills, and brooks, and lanes, and meadows, do you know
Where I shall find my little friends of forty years ago?
You see I'm old and weary, and I've traveled long and far;
I am looking for my playmates—I wonder where they are!

MEDIAEVAL EVENTIDE SONG

Come hither, lyttel chylde, and lie upon my breast to-night,
For yonder fares an angell yclad in raimaunt white,
And yonder sings ye angell, as onely angells may,
And hys songe ben of a garden that bloometh farre awaye.

To them that have no lyttel chylde Godde sometimes sendeth down
A lyttel chylde that ben a lyttel lampkyn of His own,
And, if soe be they love that chylde, He willeth it to staye,
But, elsewise, in His mercie He taketh it awaye.

And, sometimes, though they love it, Godde yearneth for ye chylde,
And sendeth angells singing whereby it ben beguiled—
They fold their arms about ye lamb that croodleth at his playe
And bear him to ye garden that bloometh farre awaye.

I wolde not lose ye lyttel lamb that Godde hath lent to me—
If I colde sing that angell songe, hoy joysome I sholde bee!
For, with my arms about him my music in his eare,
What angell songe of paradize soever sholde I feare?

Soe come, my lyttel chylde, and lie upon my breast to-night,
For yonder fares an angell, yclad in raimaunt white,
And yonder sings that angell, as onely angells may,
And hys songe ben of a garden that bloometh farre awaye.

Krinken was a little child—
It was summer when he smiled;
Oft the hoary sea and grim
Stretched its white arms out to him,
Calling: "Sun-Child, come to me,
Let me warm my heart with thee"—
But the child heard not the sea
Calling, yearning evermore
For the summer on the shore.

Krinken on the beach one day
Saw a maiden Nis at play—
On the pebbly beach she played
In the summer Krinken made.
Fair and very fair was she—
Just a little child was he.
"Krinken," said the maiden Nis
"Let me have a little kiss—
Just a kiss and go with me
To the summer lands that be
Down within the silver sea!"

Krinken was a little child—
By the maiden Nis beguiled,
Hand in hand with her went he—
And 'twas summer in the sea!
And the hoary sea and grim
To its bosom folded him—
Clasped and kissed the little form,
And the ocean's heart was warm.
But upon the misty shore
Winter brooded evermore.

With that winter in my heart,
Oft in dead of night I start—
Start and lift me up and weep,
For those visions in my sleep
Mind me of the yonder deep!
'Tis his face lifts from the sea—
'Tis his voice calls out to me—
Thus the winter bides with me.

Krinken was the little child
By the maiden Nis beguiled;
Oft the hoary sea and grim
Reached its longing arms to him,
Calling: "Sun-Child, come to me,

Let me warm my heart with thee!"
But the sea calls out no more
And 'tis winter on the shore—
Summer in the silver sea
Where with maiden Nis went he—
And the winter bides with me!

ARMENIAN FOLK-SONG—THE STORK

Welcome, O truant stork!
And where have you been so long?
And do you bring that grace of spring
That filleth my heart with song?

Descend upon my roof—
Bide on this ash content;
I would have you know what cruel woe
Befell me when you went.

All up in the moody sky
(A shifting threat o'er head!)
They were breaking the snow and bidding it go
Cover the beautiful dead.

Came snow on garden spot,
Came snow on mere and wold,
Came the withering breath of white robed death,
And the once warm earth was cold.

Stork, the tender rose tree,
That bloometh when you are here,
Trembled and sighed like a waiting bride—
Then drooped on a virgin bier.

But the brook that hath seen you come
Leaps forth with a hearty shout,
And the crocus peeps from the bed where it sleeps
To know what the noise is about.

Welcome, O honest friend!
And bide on my roof content;
For my heart would sing of the grace of spring,
When the winter of woe is spent.

THE VISION OF THE HOLY GRAIL

Deere Chryste, let not the cheere of earth,

To fill our hearts with heedless mirth
This holy Christmasse time;
But give us of thy heavenly cheere
That we may hold thy love most deere
And know thy peace sublime.

Full merry waxed King Pelles court
With Yuletide cheere and Yuletide sport,
And, when the board was spread,
Now wit ye well 'twas good to see
So fair and brave a companie
With Pelles at the head.

"Come hence, Elaine," King Pelles cried,
"Come hence and sit ye by my side,
For never yet, I trow,
Have gentle virtues like to thine
Been proved by sword nor pledged in wine,
Nor shall be nevermo!"

"Sweete sir, my father," quoth Elaine,
"Me it repents to give thee pain—
Yet, tarry I may not;
For I shall soond and I shall die
If I behold this companie
And see not Launcelot!

"My heart shall have no love but this—
My lips shall know no other kiss,
Save only, father, thine;
So graunt me leave to seek my bower,
The lonely chamber in the toure,
Where sleeps his child and mine."

Then frowned the King in sore despite;
"A murrain seize that traitrous knight,
For that he lies!" he cried—
"A base, unchristian paynim he,
Else, by my beard, he would not be
A recreant to his bride!

"Oh, I had liefer yield my life
Than see thee the deserted wife
Of dastard Launcelot!
Yet, an' thou hast no mind to stay,
Go with thy damosels away—
Lo, I'll detain ye not."

Her damosels in goodly train
Back to her chamber led Elaine,
And when her eyes were cast

Upon her babe, her tears did flow
And she did wail and weep as though
Her heart had like to brast.

The while she grieved the Yuletide sport
Waxed lustier in King Pelles' court,
And louder, houre by houre,
The echoes of the rout were borne
To where the lady, all forlorn,
Made moning in the toure,

"Swete Chryste," she cried, "ne let me hear
Their ribald sounds of Yuletide cheere
That mock at mine and me;
Graunt that my sore affliction cease
And give me of the heavenly peace
That comes with thoughts of thee!"

Lo, as she spake, a wondrous light
Made all that lonely chamber bright,
And o'er the infant's bed
A spirit hand, as samite pail,
Held sodaine foorth the Holy Grail
Above the infant's head.

And from the sacred golden cup
A subtle incense floated up
And filled the conscious air,
Which, when she breather, the fair Elaine
Forgot her grief, forgot her pain.
Forgot her sore despair.

And as the Grail's mysterious balm
Wrought in her heart a wondrous calm,
Great mervail 'twas to see
The sleeping child stretch one hand up
As if in dreams he held the cup
Which none mought win but he.

Through all the night King Pelles' court
Made mighty cheer and goodly sport.
Nor never recked the joy
That was vouchsafed that Christmass tide
To Launcelot's deserted bride
And to her sleeping boy.

Swete Chryste, let not the cheere of earth
To fill our hearts with heedless mirth
This present Christmasse night;
But send among us to and fro
Thy Holy Grail, that men may know

The joy withe wisdom dight.

THE DIVINE LULLABY

I hear Thy voice, dear Lord,
I hear it by the stormy sea,
When winter nights are black and wild,
And when, affright, I call to Thee;
It calms my fears and whispers me,
"Sleep well, my child."

I hear Thy voice, dear Lord,
In singing winds and falling snow,
The curfew chimes, the midnight bell,
"Sleep well, my child," it murmurs low;
"The guardian angels come and go—
O child, sleep well!"

I hear Thy voice, dear Lord,
Aye, though the singing winds be stilled,
Though hushed the tumult of the deep,
My fainting heart with anguish chilled
By Thy assuring tone is thrilled—
"Fear not, and sleep!"

Speak on—speak on, dear Lord!
And when the last dread night is near,
With doubts and fears and terrors wild,
Oh, let my soul expiring hear
Only these words of heavenly cheer,
"Sleep well, my child!"

MORTALITY

O Nicias, not for us alone
Was laughing Eros born,
Nor shines alone for us the moon,
Nor burns the ruddy morn;
Alas! to-morrow lies not in the ken
Of us who are, O Nicias, mortal men!

A FICKLE WOMAN

Her nature is the sea's, that smiles to-night
A radiant maiden in the moon's soft light;

The unsuspecting seaman sets his sails,
Forgetful of the fury of her gales;
To-morrow, mad with storms, the ocean roars,
And o'er his hapless wreck the flood she pours!

EGYPTIAN FOLK-SONG

Grim is the face that looks into the night
Over the stretch of sands;
A sullen rock in the sea of white—
A ghostly shadow in ghostly light,
Peering and moaning it stands.
"Oh, is it the king that rides this way—
Oh, is it the king that rides so free?
I have looked for the king this many a day,
But the years that mock me will not say
Why tarrieth he!"

'Tis not your king that shall ride to-night,
But a child that is fast asleep;
And the horse he shall ride is the Dream-Horse
white—
Aha, he shall speed through the ghostly light
Where the ghostly shadows creep!
"My eyes are dull and my face is sere,
Yet unto the word he gave I cling,
For he was a Pharoah that set me here—
And lo! I have waited this many a year
For him—my king!"

Oh, past thy face my darling shall ride
Swift as the burning winds that bear
The sand clouds over the desert wide—
Swift to the verdure and palms beside
The wells off there!
"And is it the mighty king I shall see
Come riding into the night?
Oh, is it the king come back to me—
Proudly and fiercely rideth he,
With centuries dight!"

I know no king but my dark-eyed dear
That shall ride the Dream-Horse white;
But see! he wakes at my bosom here,
While the Dream-Horse frettingly lingers near
To speed with my babe to-night!
And out of the desert darkness peers
A ghostly, ghastly, shadowy thing
Like a spirit come out of the moldering years,

And ever that waiting specter hears
The coming king!

ARMENIAN FOLK-SONG—THE PARTRIDGE

As beats the sun from mountain crest,
With "pretty, pretty",
Cometh the partridge from her nest;
The flowers threw kisses sweet to her
(For all the flowers that bloomed knew her);
Yet hasteneth she to mine and me—
Ah! pretty, pretty;
Ah! dear little partridge!

And when I hear the partridge cry
So pretty, pretty,
Upon the house-top, breakfast I;
She comes a-chirping far and wide,
And swinging from the mountain side—
I see and hear the dainty dear!
Ah! pretty, pretty;
Ah! dear little partridge!

Thy nest's inlaid with posies rare.
And pretty, pretty
Bloom violet, rose, and lily there;
The place is full of balmy dew
(The tears of flowers in love with you!)
And one and all impassioned call;
"O pretty, pretty—
O dear little partridge!"

Thy feathers they are soft and sleek—
So pretty, pretty!
Long is thy neck and small thy breast;
The color of thy plumage far
More bright than rainbow colors are!
Sweeter than dove is she I love—
My pretty, pretty—
My dear little partridge!

When comes the partridge from the tree,
So pretty, pretty!
And sings her little hymn to me,
Why, all the world is cheered thereby—
The heart leaps up into the eye,
And echo then gives back again
Our "Pretty, pretty,"
Our "Dear little partridge!"

Admitting the most blest of all
And pretty, pretty,
The birds come with thee at thy call;
In flocks they come and round they play,
And this is what they seem to say—
They say and sing, each feathered thing;
"Ah! pretty, pretty;
Ah! dear little partridge!"

ALASKAN BALLADRY, NO. 1

The Northland reared his hoary head
And spied the Southland leagues away—
"Fairest of all fair brides," he said,
"Be thou my bride, I pray!"

Whereat the Southland laughed and cried
"I'll bide beside my native sea,
And I shall never be thy bride
'Til thou com'st wooing me!"

The Northland's heart was a heart of ice,
A diamond glacier, mountain high—
Oh, love is sweet at my price,
As well know you and I!

So gayly the Northland took his heart;
And cast it in the wailing sea—
"Go, thou, with all my cunning art
And woo my bride for me!"

For many a night and for many a day,
And over the leagues that rolled between
The true heart messenger sped away
To woo the Southland queen.

But the sea wailed loud, and the sea wailed long
While ever the Northland cried in glee:
"Oh, thou shalt sing us our bridal song,
When comes my bride, O sea!"

At the foot of the Southland's golden throne
The heart of the Northland ever throbs—
For that true heart speaks in the waves that moan
The songs that it sings are sobs.

Ever the Southland spurns the cries
Of the messenger pleading the Northland's part—

The summer shines in the Southland's eyes—
The winter bides in her heart.

And ever unto that far-off place
Which love doth render a hallow spot,
The Northland turneth his honest face
And wonders she cometh not.

The sea wails loud, and the sea wails long,
As the ages of waiting drift slowly by,
But the sea shall sing no bridal song—
As well know you and I!

OLD DUTCH LOVE SONG

I am not rich, and yet my wealth
Surpasseth human measure;
My store untold
Is not of gold
Nor any sordid treasure.
Let this one hoard his earthly pelf,
Another court ambition—
Not for a throne
Would I disown
My poor and proud condition!

The worldly gain achieved to-day
To-morrow may be flying—
The gifts of kings
Are fleeting things—
The gifts of love undying!
In her I love is all my wealth—
For her my sole endeavor;
No heart, I ween,
Hath fairer queen,
No liege such homage, ever!

AN ECLOGUE FROM VIRGIL

(The exile Meliboeus finds Tityrus in possession of his own farm, restored to him by the emperor
Augustus, and a conversation ensues. The poem is in praise of Augustus, peace and pastoral life)

Meliboeus
Tityrus, all in the shade of the wide-spreading beech tree reclining,
Sweet is that music you've made on your pipe that is oaten and slender;
Exiles from home, you beguile our hearts from their hopeless repining,
As you sing Amaryllis the while in pastorals tuneful and tender.

Tityrus
A god—yes, a god, I declare—vouchsafes me these pleasant conditions,
And often I gayly repair with a tender white lamb to his altar,
He gives me the leisure to play my greatly admired compositions,
While my heifers go browsing all day, unhampered of bell and halter.

Meliboeus
I do not begrudge you repose; I simply admit I'm confounded
To find you unscathed of the woes of pillage and tumult and battle;
To exile and hardship devote and by merciless enemies hounded,
I drag at this wretched old goat and coax on my famishing cattle.
Oh, often the omens presaged the horrors which now overwhelm me—
But, come, if not elsewise engaged, who is this good deity, tell me!

Tityrus (reminiscently)
The city—the city called Rome, with, my head full of herding and tillage,
I used to compare with my home, these pastures wherein you now wander;
But I didn't take long to find out that the city surpasses the village
As the cypress surpasses the sprout that thrives in the thicket out
yonder.

Meliboeus
Tell me, good gossip, I pray, what led you to visit the city?

Tityrus
Liberty! which on a day regarded my lot with compassion
My age and distresses, forsooth, compelled that proud mistress to pity,
That had snubbed the attentions of youth in most reprehensible fashion.
Oh, happy, thrice happy, the day when the cold Galatea forsook me,
And equally happy, I say, the hour when that other girl took me!

Meliboeus (slyly, as if addressing the damsel)
So now, Amaryllis the truth of your ill-disguised grief I discover!
You pined for a favorite youth with cityfied damsels hobnobbing.
And soon your surroundings partook of your grief for your recusant lover—
The pine trees, the copse and the brook for Tityrus ever went sobbing.

Tityrus
Meliboeus, what else could I do? Fate doled me no morsel of pity;
My toil was all in vain the year through, no matter how earnest or clever,
Till, at last, came that god among men—that king from that wonderful city,
And quoth: "Take your homesteads again—they are yours and your assigns forever!"

Meliboeus
Happy, oh, happy old man! rich in what's better than money—
Rich in contentment, you can gather sweet peace by mere listening;
Bees with soft murmurings go hither and thither for honey.
Cattle all gratefully low in pastures where fountains are glistening—
Hark! in the shade of that rock the pruner with singing rejoices—
The dove in the elm and the flock of wood-pigeons hoarsely repining,

The plash of the sacred cascade—ah, restful, indeed, are these voices,
Tityrus, all in the shade of your wide-spreading beech-tree reclining!

Tityrus
And he who insures this to me—oh, craven I were not to love him!
Nay, rather the fish of the sea shall vacate the water they swim in,
The stag quit his bountiful grove to graze in the ether above him.
While folk antipodean rove along with their children and women!

Meliboeus (suddenly recalling his own misery)
But we who are exiled must go; and whither—ah, whither—God knoweth!
Some into those regions of snow or of desert where Death reigneth only;
Some off to the country of Crete, where rapid Oaxes down floweth.
And desperate others retreat to Britain, the bleak isle and lonely.
Dear land of my birth! shall I see the horde of invaders oppress thee?
Shall the wealth that outspringeth from thee by the hand of the alien be squandered?
Dear cottage wherein I was born! shall another in conquest possess thee—
Another demolish in scorn the fields and the groves where I've wandered?
My flock! never more shall you graze on that furze-covered hillside above me—
Gone, gone are the halcyon days when my reed piped defiance to sorrow!
Nevermore in the vine-covered grot shall I sing of the loved ones that love me—
Let yesterday's peace be forgot in dread of the stormy to-morrow!

Tityrus
But rest you this night with me here; my bed—we will share it together,
As soon as you've tasted my cheer, my apples and chestnuts and cheeses;
The evening a'ready is nigh—the shadows creep over the heather,
And the smoke is rocked up to the sky to the lullaby song of the
breezes.

HORACE TO MAECENAS

How breaks my heart to hear you say
You feel the shadows fall about you!
The gods forefend
That fate, O friend!
I would not, I could not live without you!
You gone, what would become of me,
Your shadow, O beloved Maecenas?
We've shared the mirth—
And sweets of earth—
Let's share the pangs of death between us!

I should not dread Chinaera's breath
Nor any threat of ghost infernal;
Nor fear nor pain
Should part us twain—
For so have willed the powers eternal.
No false allegiance have I sworn,

And, whatsoever fate betide you,
Mine be the part
To cheer your heart—
With loving song to fare beside you!

Love snatched you from the claws of death
And gave you to the grateful city;
The falling tree
That threatened me
Did Fannus turn aside in pity;
With horoscopes so wondrous like,
Why question that we twain shall wander,
As in this land,
So, hand in hand,
Into the life that waiteth yonder?

So to your shrine, O patron mine,
With precious wine and victims fare you;
Poor as I am,
A humble lamb
Must testify what love I bear you.
But to the skies shall sweetly rise
The sacrifice from shrine and heather,
And thither bear
The solemn prayer
That, when we go, we go together!

HORACE'S "SAILOR AND SHADE"

Sailor
You, who have compassed land and sea
Now all unburied lie;
All vain your store of human lore,
For you were doomed to die.
The sire of Pelops likewise fell,
Jove's honored mortal guest—
So king and sage of every age
At last lie down to rest.
Plutonian shades enfold the ghost
Of that majestic one
Who taught as truth that he, forsooth,
Had once been Pentheus' son;
Believe who may, he's passed away
And what he did is done.
A last night comes alike to all—
One path we all must tread,
Through sore disease or stormy seas
Or fields with corpses red—
Whate'er our deeds that pathway leads

To regions of the dead.

Shade
The fickle twin Illyrian gales
O'erwhelmed me on the wave—
But that you live, I pray you give
My bleaching bones a grave!
Oh, then when cruel tempests rage
You all unharmed shall be—
Jove's mighty hand shall guard by land
And Neptune's on the sea.
Perchance you fear to do what shall
Bring evil to your race.
Or, rather fear that like me here
You'll lack a burial place.
So, though you be in proper haste,
Bide long enough I pray,
To give me, friend, what boon will send
My soul upon its way!

UHLAND'S "CHAPEL"

Yonder stands the hillside chapel,
'Mid the evergreens and rocks,
All day long it hears the song
Of the shepherd to his flocks.

Then the chapel bell goes tolling—
Knolling for a soul that's sped;
Silent and sad the shepherd lad
Hears the requiem for the dead.

Shepherd, singers of the valley,
Voiceless now, speed on before;
Soon shall knell that chapel bell
For the songs you'll sing no more.

"THE HAPPY ISLES" OF HORACE

Oh, come with me to the Happy Isles
In the golden haze off yonder,
Where the song of the sun-kissed breeze beguiles
And the ocean loves to wander.

Fragrant the vines that mantle those hills,
Proudly the fig rejoices,
Merrily dance the virgin rills,

Blending their myriad voices.

Our herds shall suffer no evil there,
But peacefully feed and rest them—
Never thereto shall prowling bear
Or serpent come to molest them.

Neither shall Eurus, wanton bold,
Nor feverish drought distress us,
But he that compasseth heat and cold
Shall temper them both to bless us.

There no vandal foot has trod,
And the pirate hordes that wander
Shall never profane the sacred sod
Of these beautiful isles out yonder.

Never a spell shall blight our vines
Nor Sirius blaze above us.
But you and I shall drink our wines
And sing to the loved that love us.

So come with me where fortune smiles
And the gods invite devotion—
Oh, come with me to the Happy Isles
In the haze of that far-off ocean!

HORATIAN LYRICS

I

Odes I, 11

What end the gods may have ordained for me,
And what for thee,
Seek not to learn, Leuconoe; we may not know;
Chaldean tables cannot bring us rest—
'Tis for the best
To bear in patience what may come, or weal or woe.

If for more winters our poor lot is cast,
Or this the last,
Which on the crumbling rocks has dashed Etruscan seas;
Strain clear the wine—this life is short, at best;
Take hope with zest,
And, trusting not To-Morrow, snatch To-Day for ease!

II

Odes I, 23

Why do you shun me, Chloe, like the fawn,
That, fearful of the breezes and the wood,
Has sought her timorous mother since the dawn
And on the pathless mountain tops has stood?

Her trembling heart a thousand fears invites—
Her sinking knees with nameless terrors shake;
Whether the rustling leaf of spring affrights,
Or the green lizards stir the slumbering brake.

I do not follow with a tigerish thought
Or with the fierce Gaetulian lion's quest;
So, quickly leave your mother, as you ought,
Full ripe to nestle on a husband's breast.

HORACE II, 13

O fountain of Blandusia,
Whence crystal waters flow,
With garlands gay and wine I'll pay
The sacrifice I owe;
A sportive kid with budding horns
I have, whose crimson blood
Anon shall die and sanctify
Thy cool and babbling flood.

O fountain of Blandusia,
The dogstar's hateful spell
No evil brings unto the springs
That from thy bosom well;
Here oxen, wearied by the plow,
The roving cattle here,
Hasten in quest of certain rest
And quaff thy gracious cheer.

O fountain of Blandusia,
Ennobled shalt thou be,
For I shall sing the joys that spring
Beneath your ilex tree;
Yes, fountain of Blandusia,
Posterity shall know
The cooling brooks that from thy nooks
Singing and dancing go!

Come, Phyllis, I've a cask of wine
That fairly reeks with precious juices.
And in your tresses you shall twine
The loveliest flowers this vale produces.

My cottage wears a gracious smile—
The altar decked in floral glory,—
Yearns for the lamb which bleats the while
As though it pined for honors gory.

Hither our neighbors nimbly fare—
The boys agog, the maidens snickering,
And savory smells possess the air
As skyward kitchen flames are flickering.

You ask what means this grand display,
This festive throng and goodly diet?
Well—since you're bound to have your way—
I don't mind telling on the quiet.

'Tis April 13, as you know—
A day and month devote to Venus,
Whereon was born some years ago,
My very worthy friend, Macenas.

Nay, pay no heed to Telephus—
Your friends agree he doesn't love you;
The way he flirts convinces us
He really is not worthy of you!

Aurora's son, unhappy lad!
You know the fate that overtook him?
And Pegasus a rider had—
I say he had before he shook him!

Haec docet (as you may agree):
'Tis meet that Phyllis should discover
A wisdom in preferring me
And mittening every other lover.

So come, O Phyllis, last and best
Of loves with which this heart's been smitten;
Come, sing my jealous fears to rest—
And let your songs be those I've written.

HUGO'S "POOL IN THE FOREST"

How calm, how beauteous, and how cool—
How like a sister to the skies,
Appears the broad, transparent pool
That in this quiet forest lies.
The sunshine ripples on its face,
And from the world around, above,
It hath caught down the nameless grace
Of such reflections as we love.

But deep below its surface crawl
The reptile horrors of the Night—
The dragons, lizards, serpents—all
The hideous brood that hate the Light;
Through poison fern and slimy weed,
And under ragged, jagged stones
They scuttle, or, in ghoulish greed,
They lap a dead man's bones.

And as, O pool, thou dost cajole
With seemings that beguile us well,
So doeth many a human soul
That teemeth with the lusts of hell.

HORACE I, 4

'Tis spring! the boats bound to the sea;
The breezes, loitering kindly over
The fields, again bring herds and men
The grateful cheer of honeyed clover.

Now Venus hither leads her train,
The Nymphs and Graces join in orgies,
The moon is bright and by her light
Old Vulcan kindles up his forges.

Bind myrtle now about your brow,
And weave fair flowers in maiden tresses—
Appease God Pan, who, kind to man,
Our fleeting life with affluence blesses.

But let the changing seasons mind us
That Death's the certain doom of mortals—
Grim Death who waits at humble gat
And likewise stalks through kingly portals.

Soon, Sestius, shall Plutonian shades
Enfold you with their hideous seemings—
Then love and mirth and joys of earth
Shall fade away like fevered dreamings.

LOVE SONG—HEINE

Many a beauteous flower doth spring
From the tears that flood my eyes,
And the nightingale doth sing
In the burthen of my sighs.

If, O child, thou lovest me,
Take these flowerets, fair and frail,
And my soul shall waft to thee
Love songs of the nightingale.

HORACE II, 3

Be tranquil, Dellius, I pray;
For though you pine your life away
With dull complaining breath,
Or speed with song and wine each day—
Still, still your doom is death.

Where the white poplar and the pine
In glorious arching shade combine
And the brook singing goes,
Bid them bring store of nard and wine
And garlands of the rose.

Let's live while chance and youth obtain—
Soon shall you quit this fair domain
Kissed by the Tiber's gold,
And all your earthly pride and gain
Some heedless heir shall hold.

One ghostly boat shall some time bear
From scenes of mirthfulness or care
Each fated human soul!—
Shall waft and leave his burden where
The waves of Lethe roll.

So come, I pri' thee, Dellius, mine—
Let's sing our songs and drink our wine
In that sequestered nook
Where the white poplar and the pine
Stand listening to the brook.

THE TWO COFFINS

In yonder old cathedral
Two lonely coffins lie;
In one the head of the state lies dead,
And a singer sleeps hard by.

Once had that king great power,
And proudly he ruled the land—
His crown e'en now is on his brow
And his sword is in his hand!

How sweetly sleeps the singer
With calmly folded eyes,
And on the breast of the bard at rest
The harp that he sounded lies.

The castle walls are falling
And war distracts the land,
But the sword leaps not from that mildewed spot—
There in that dead king's hand!

But with every grace of nature
There seems to float along—
To cheer the hearts of men—
The singer's deathless song!

HORACE I, 31

As forth he pours the new made wine,
What blessing asks the lyric poet—
What boon implores in this fair shrine
Of one full likely to bestow it?

Not for Sardinia's plenteous store,
Nor for Calabrian herds he prayeth,
Nor yet for India's wealth galore,
Nor meads where voiceless Liris playeth.

Let honest riches celebrate
The harvest earned—I'd not deny it;
Yet am I pleased with my estate,
My humble home, my frugal diet.

Child of Latonia, this I crave;
May peace of mind and health attend me,
And down into my very grave
May this dear lyre of mine befriend me!

HORACE TO HIS LUTE

If ever in the sylvan shade
A song immortal we have made,
Come now, O lute, I pri' thee come—
Inspire a song of Latium.

A Lesbian first thy glories proved—
In arms and in repose he loved
To sweep thy dulcet strings and raise
His voice in Love's and Liber's praise;
The Muses, too, and him who clings
To Mother Venus' apron-strings,
And Lycus beautiful, he sung
In those old days when you were young.

O shell, that art the ornament
Of Phoebus, bringing sweet content
To Jove, and soothing troubles all—
Come and requite me, when I call!

HORACE I, 22

Fuscus, whoso to good inclines—
And is a faultless liver—
Nor moorish spear nor bow need fear,
Nor poison-arrowed quiver.

Ay, though through desert wastes he roams,
Or scales the rugged mountains,
Or rests beside the murmuring tide
Of weird Hydaspan fountains!

Lo, on a time, I gayly paced
The Sabine confines shady,
And sung in glee of Lalage,
My own and dearest lady.

And, as I sung, a monster wolf
Slunk through the thicket from me—
But for that song, as I strolled along
He would have overcome me!

Set me amid those poison mists
Which no fair gale dispelleth,
Or in the plains where silence reigns
And no thing human dwelleth;

Still shall I love my Lalage—
Still sing her tender graces;
And, while I sing my theme shall bring
Heaven to those desert places!

THE "ARS POETICA" OF HORACE

XXIII

I love the lyric muse!
For when mankind ran wild in groves,
Came holy Orpheus with his songs
And turned men's hearts from bestial loves,
From brutal force and savage wrongs;
Came Amphion, too, and on his lyre
Made such sweet music all the day
That rocks, instinct with warm desire,
Pursued him in his glorious way.

I love the lyric muse!
Hers was the wisdom that of yore
Taught man the rights of fellow-man—
Taught him to worship God the more
And to revere love's holy ban;
Hers was the hand that jotted down
The laws correcting divers wrongs—
And so came honor and renown
To bards and to their noble songs.

I love the lyric muse!
Old Homer sung unto the lyre,
Tyrtaeus, too, in ancient days—
Still, warmed by their immortal fire,
How doth our patriot spirit blaze!
The oracle, when questioned, sings—
So we our way in life are taught;
In verse we soothe the pride of kings,
In verse the drama has been wrought.

I love the lyric muse!
Be not ashamed, O noble friend,
In honest gratitude to pay
Thy homage to the gods that send
This boon to charm all ill away.
With solemn tenderness revere
This voiceful glory as a shrine
Wherein the quickened heart may hear
The counsels of a voice divine!

MARTHY'S YOUNKIT

The mountain brook sung lonesomelike
And loitered on its way
Ez if it waited for a child
To jine it in its play;
The wild flowers of the hillside
Bent down their heads to hear
The music of the little feet
That had, somehow, grown so dear;
The magpies, like winged shadders,
Wuz a-flutterin' to and fro
Among the rocks and holler stumps
In the ragged gulch below;
The pines 'nd hemlock tosst their boughs
(Like they wuz arms) 'nd made
Soft, sollum music on the slope
Where he had often played.
But for these lonesome, sollum voices
On the mountain side,
There wuz no sound the summer day
That Marthy's younkit died.

We called him Marthy's younkit,
For Marthy wuz the name
Uv her ez wuz his mar, the wife
Uv Sorry Tom—the same
Ez taught the school-house on the hill
Way back in sixty-nine
When she married Sorry Tom wich ownt
The Gosh-all-Hemlock mine;
And Marthy's younkit wuz their first,
Wich, bein' how it meant
The first on Red Hoss mountain,
Wuz trooly a event!
The miners sawed off short on work
Es soon ez they got word
That Dock Devine allowed to Casey
What had just occurred;
We loaded 'nd whooped around
Until we all wuz hoarse,
Salutin' the arrival,
Wich weighed ten pounds, uv course!

Three years, and sech a pretty child!
His mother's counterpart—
Three years, and sech a holt ez he
Had got on every heart!

A peert and likely little tyke
With hair ez red ez gold,
A laughin', toddlin' everywhere—
And only three years old!
Up yonder, sometimes, to the store,
And sometimes down the hill
He kited (boys is boys, you know—
You couldn't keep him still!)
And there he'd play beside the brook
Where purpel wild flowers grew
And the mountain pines 'nd hemlocks
A kindly shadder threw
And sung soft, sollum toons to him,
While in the gulch below
The magpies, like strange sperrits,
Went flutterin' to and fro.

Three years, and then the fever come;
It wuzn't right, you know,
With all us old ones in the camp,
For that little child to go!
It's right the old should die, but that
A harmless little child
Should miss the joy uv life 'nd love—
That can't be reconciled!
That's what we thought that summer day,
And that is what we said
Ez we looked upon the piteous face
Uv Marthy's younkit dead;
But for his mother sobbin'
The house wuz very still,
And Sorry Tom wuz lookin' through
The winder down the hill
To the patch beneath the hemlocks
Where his darlin' used to play,
And the mountain brook sung lonesomelike
And loitered on its way.

A preacher come from Roarin' Forks
To comfort 'em 'nd pray,
And all the camp wuz present
At the obsequies next day,
A female teacher staged it twenty miles
To sing a hymn,
And we jined her in the chorus—
Big, husky men 'nd grim
Sung "Jesus, Lover uv my Soul,"
And then the preacher prayed
And preacht a sermon on the death
Uv that fair blossom laid
Among them other flow'rs he loved—

Which sermon set sech weight
On sinners bein' always heelt
Against the future state
That, though it had been fash'nable
To swear a perfect streak,
There warnt no swearin' in the camp
For pretty nigh a week!

Last thing uv all, six strappin' men
Took up the little load
And bore it tenderly along
The windin' rocky road
To where the coroner had dug
A grave beside the brook—
In sight uv Marthy's winder, where
The same could set and look
And wonder if his cradle in
That green patch long 'nd wide
Wuz ez soothin' ez the cradle that
Wuz empty at her side;
And wonder of the mournful songs
The pines wuz singin' then
Wuz ez tender ez the lullabies
She'd never sing again;
And if the bosom uv the earth
In which he lay at rest
Wuz half ez lovin' 'nd ez warm
Ez wuz his mother's breast.

The camp is gone, but Red Hoss mountain
Rears its kindly head
And looks down sort uv tenderly,
Upon its cherished dead;
And I reckon that, through all the years
That little boy wich died
Sleeps sweetly 'nd contentedly
Upon the mountain-side;
That the wild flowers of the summer time
Bend down their heads to hear
The footfall uv a little friend they
Know not slumbers near;
That the magpies on the sollum rocks
Strange flutterin' shadders make.
And the pines 'nd hemlocks wonder that
The sleeper doesn't wake;
That the mountain brook sings lonesomelike
And loiters on its way
Ez if it waited f'r a child
To jine it in its play.

ABU MIDJAN

"When Father Time swings round his scythe,
Intomb me 'neath the bounteous vine,
So that its juices, red and blithe,
May cheer these thirsty bones of mine.

"Elsewise with tears and bated breath
Should I survey the life to be.
But oh! How should I hail the death
That brings that vinous grace to me!"

So sung the dauntless Saracen,
Whereat the Prophet-Chief ordains
That, curst of Allah, loathed of men,
The faithless one shall die in chains.

But one vile Christian slave that lay
A prisoner near that prisoner saith;
"God willing, I will plant some day
A vine where thou liest in death."

Lo, over Abu Midjan's grave
With purpling fruit a vine-tree grows;
Where rots the martyred Christian slave
Allah, and only Allah, knows!

THE DYING YEAR

The year has been a tedious one—
A weary round of toil and sorrow,
And, since it now at last is gone,
We say farewell and hail the morrow.

Yet o'er the wreck which time has wrought
A sweet, consoling ray is shimmered—
The one but compensating thought
That literary life has glimmered.

Struggling with hunger and with cold
The world contemptuously beheld 'er;
The little thing was one year old—
But who'd have cared had she been elder?

DEAD ROSES

He placed a rose in my nut-brown hair—
A deep red rose with a fragrant heart
And said: "We'll set this day apart,
So sunny, so wondrous fair."

His face was full of a happy light,
His voice was tender and low and sweet,
The daisies and the violets grew at our feet—
Alas, for the coming of night!

The rose is black and withered and dead!
'Tis hid in a tiny box away;
The nut-brown hair is turning to gray,
And the light of the day is fled!

The light of the beautiful day is fled,
Hush'd is the voice so sweet and low—
And I—ah, me! I loved him so—
And the daisies grow over his head!

Eugene Field – A Short Biography

Eugene Field was born on 2nd September, 1850 in St. Louis, Missouri at 634 S. Broadway to parents Roswell Martin and Frances Reed Field, both of New England stock. Tragically Field lost his mother at age 6 and was thereafter brought up by a cousin, Mary Field French, in Amherst, Massachusetts.

Field attended Williams College in Williamstown, Massachusetts.

When he was 19 his father died, and Field dropped out of Williams. Field's father, Roswell Martin Field, was the lawyer for Dred Scott, the slave who famously sued for his freedom. The complaint was sometimes referred to as 'The lawsuit that started the Civil War'.

Field then went to Knox College in Galesburg, Illinois, but again dropped out. This time after a year. However he did then summon himself to attend the University of Missouri in Columbia, Missouri, where his brother Roswell was studying. As can be gathered from his efforts to date Field was not the most serious of students but was gaining the reputation of being a prankster. Among his more outlandish attempts were a raid on the president's wine cellar, painting the president's house in school colors, and firing the school's landmark cannons at midnight.

Field tried acting but found it not to his liking, studied law but with little success, but did have an interest in writing for the student newspaper.

When his studies finished in 1871, although he never graduated, he collected his share of his inheritance from his father's estate, and set off for a trip to explore Europe. After six months, with funds from the inheritance exhausted, he returned to the United States.

Field then set to work as a journalist for the St. Joseph Gazette in Saint Joseph, Missouri, in 1875.

That same year he married the sixteen-year-old Julia Sutherland Comstock of St Joseph, Missouri. They would eventually have eight children during their twenty-two years of marriage, of whom only five would reach adulthood. Field, knowing that his understanding of finances was somewhat poor, arranged for all the money he earned to be sent to his wife for her to administer on behalf of the family.

In his career as a journalist he soon found a niche that suited him. His articles were light, humorous and written in a personal and gossipy style that endeared him to his readership. Some were soon being syndicated to other newspapers around the States. Field rose to be the city editor of the Gazette.

From 1876 through 1880, the Family lived in St. Louis. Field worked initially as an editorial writer for the Morning Journal and then for the Times-Journal. From there he worked for a short time as the managing editor of the Kansas City Times before settling, for two years, as the editor of the Denver Tribune. He also wrote a column for the paper, 'Odds and Ends,' poking fun at the climate, the muddy roads, the frontier language, and other aspects of Denver life. However his readership was large and growing. Further opportunities would come.

In 1883 the Field moved the family to Chicago lured by a salary of $50 a week. Field now began work for the Chicago Daily News. Here he wrote his humorous newspaper column called Sharps and Flats. He quickly found out that $50 dollars in Denver didn't stretch that far in bustling Chicago.

His column ran in the newspaper's morning edition. In it Field made quips about issues and personalities of the day, especially regarding the arts and literature. His pet subject was the intellectual superiority of Chicago, especially when he compared it to Boston, which he often did. In April 1887, he wrote, "While Chicago is humping herself in the interests of literature, art and the sciences, vain old Boston is frivoling away her precious time in an attempted renaissance of the cod fisheries."

In another article that year after Chicago's National League baseball club sold future baseball Hall of Famer Mike "King" Kelly to Boston which overlapped with a speaking tour visit from the famous Boston poet and diplomat James Russell Lowell he wrote: "Chicago feels a special interest in Mr. Lowell at this particular time because he is perhaps the foremost representative of the enterprising and opulent community which within the last week has secured the services of one of Chicago's honored sons for the base-ball season of 1887. The fact that Boston has come to Chicago for the captain of her baseball nine has reinvigorated the bonds of affection between the metropolis of the Bay state and the metropolis of the mighty west; the truth of this will appear in the mighty welcome which our public will give Mr. Lowell next Tuesday."

It was in 1888 that his poem 'Little Boy Blue' was printed in America, a weekly journal. It achieved for Field instant and lasting fame. Coincidentally the same issue carried a poem by James Russell Lowell. Field was immensely pleased that his own poem was regarded with considerably more weight and acclaim.

Field had first published poetry in 1879, when his poem 'Christmas Treasures' was published. It later appeared in 'A Little Book of Western Verse' (1889). This was the beginning that would eventually number over a dozen volumes. He developed a style of light-hearted poems for children. Among the perennial favorites are 'Wynken, Blynken, and Nod' and 'The Duel' (but better known as 'The Gingham Dog and the Calico Cat') and 'Little Boy Blue' about the death of a child. As well as verse Field published an extensive range of short stories including 'The Holy Cross' and 'Daniel and the Devil.'

Field treasured rare, unusual and beautiful books and his personal library had scores of them. He also enjoyed making them too and frequently worked long hours with great care and various colored inks decorating the first letter of his poems.

In 1889 whilst the family were in London and Field himself was recovering from a bout of ill health he wrote his most famous poem; 'Lovers Lane'. It is often thought to have been written whilst the couple were courting but recent research settles it authorship to this later date. The poem was written as a reminder of better days when the couple courted in her father's buggy on 'Lover's Lane, St Jo'.

Field was ever curious and keen to push his boundaries. In 1891 with his brother Roswell they wrote and published 'Echoes from the Sabine Farm' a loosely translated version of Horace.

On 4th November 1895 Eugene Field Sr died in Chicago of a heart attack at the age of 45. He is buried at the Church of the Holy Comforter in Kenilworth, Illinois.

The New York Times described his death: CHICAGO, Nov. 4. — Eugene Field, the poet and humorist, died at 5 o'clock this morning of heart disease at his residence in Buena Park. Although Mr. Field had been ill for the past three days, his sudden death was totally unexpected.

Field was originally interred at Graceland Cemetery in Chicago, but his son-in-law, Senior Warden of the Church of the Holy Comforter, had him reinterred on 7th March, 1926.

Several of his poems were set to music with commercial success. Many of his works were accompanied by paintings from the exceptional talents of Maxfield Parrish.

During his lifetime he was often referred to as the 'poet of childhood'. This may account for his anonymous publication of 'Only a Boy'. In our own times the work would probably be frowned upon. It concerns a 12-year-old boy being seduced by a woman in her 30s. The 1920's drama critic/magazine editor George Jean Nathan claimed it was a popular but forbidden work among those coming of age in the early 1900's.

Much of what Field wrote was light, humourous and of its time. And that is perhaps why it has endured. Its writes of a time that, in his words, suspends itself from the harsh reality of real life to a gentler and more touching time that exists in the imagination.

Eugene Field – A Concise Bibliography

The Tribune Primer (1882)
Culture's Garland (1887)
A Little Book of Profitable Tales (1889)
A Little Book of Western Verse (1889)
With Trumpet and Drum (1892)
Echoes from the Sabine Farm (1893)
The Holy Cross and Other Tales (1893)
Second Book of Verse (1893)
Love Songs of Childhood (1894)
Love Affairs of a Bibliomaniac (1895)

Little Willie (1895)
Songs and Other Verse (1896)
Second Book of Tales (1896)
The House; An Episode in the Lives of Reuben Baker, Astronomer and His Wife Alice (1896)
Field Flowers (1896)
Florence Bardsley's Story (1897)
Lullaby Songs of Childhood (1897)
Lullaby Land (1898)
Sharps and Flats (1900)
The Stars (1901)
Nonsense for Old and Young (1901)
A Little Book of Nonsense (1901)
A Little Book of Tribune Verse (1901)
The Sabine Farm (1903)
John Smith USA (1905)
The Clink of Ice (1905)
Hoosier Lyrics (1905)
Cradle Lullabies (1909)
The Poems of Eugene Field (1910)
Christmas Tales and Christmas Verse (1912)
Penn-Yan Bill's Wooing (1914)
The Yankee Abroad (1917)
The Mouse and the Moonbeam (1919)
Poems of Childhood (1920)
The Gingham Dog and the Calico Cat (1926)
Child Verses (1927)
The Sugar Plum Tree (1929)
In Wink-a-way Land (1930)

www.ingramcontent.com/pod-product-compliance
Lightning Source LLC
Chambersburg PA
CBHW060051050426
42448CB00011B/2397